Music Minus One Alto Saxophone

Glenn Zottola plays...

Classic
Arrangements

for Alto Saxophone

with Full Orchestral Accompaniments
Original Transcriptions
Inspired by Frank Sinatra

- notes continued from back cover

One tune that will forever be associated with Sinatra, is Harold Arlen's immortal *"Come Rain or Come Shine"* first recorded by the singer back in 1961 and becoming a staple ever since. Known for Don Costa's string and horn arrangements, the saxophonist and band stay true to the original treatment resulting in a splendid version conjuring up memories of the Sinatra of old. Though Josef Myrow wrote the song *"You Make Me Feel So Young,"* it was Mack Gordon's lyrics that made this a Sinatra favorite and here, Zottola's masterful solo sound rides Riddle's horn and ensemble arrangement in a wonderfully delicious interpretation.

The Rube Bloom/Ted Koehler song *"Don't Worry 'Bout Me"* from 1938, is one of Sinatra's most under- appreciated and less recognized ballads first recorded by him in his 1956 *This Is Sinatra!* Not mincing words or lyrics for that matter, the music on this piece is, simply brief but beautifully done. The Harry M. Woods pop classic *"Try A Little Tenderness"* made so popular by the great Otis Redding, has actually been recorded many times by many singers among them, Sinatra. Here, Zottola presents a warm string-laden rendition leading the music with a soft touch on the alto as he, dare I say it, does indeed, "try a little tenderness."

On the pulsating side, there's Ralph Rainger's *"If I Should Lose You,"* a Quincy Jones Big Band arrangement full of swing and power-play, followed by an aggressive string section on the beautiful *"Autumn In New York"* where the saxophonist draws on the original Billy May arrangement in reprising the splendor of the oft-recorded jazz standard performed by the singer in 1963 and voiced by Sinatra in many concerts and events thereafter. The album closes on the swinging side reprising the 1932 Victor Young classic *"Street of Dreams"* where Zottola is at his propulsive best belting out the melody with gusto. This one, may well be the Instrumental version of the 1966 Sinatra live recording with the great Count Basie entitled *Sinatra At The Sands.*

There is so much more music that one can associate with arguably, the greatest singer of our time that this excellent musical statement may seem inadequate in describing the essence of Sinatra's legacy. Nevertheless, *Alto/Sinatra* is an exceptional offering capturing some of the legend's best songs in an instrumental setting with Glenn Zottola's alto saxophone singing the melodies with an ensemble accompaniment that's "alto-riffect." It is another dream come true for Zottola, marrying the big band music of Frank Sinatra with the soaring alto saxophone solos in the lead. As Glenn states "Charlie Parker meets Sinatra," though it may never have happened, this is the closest one will get to that experience.

Edward Blanco,
Jazz critic with All About Jazz, producer and host at WDNA jazz radio in Miami, FL.

Music Minus One
50 Executive Boulevard • Elmsford, New York 10523-1325
914-592-1188 • e-mail: info@musicminusone.com
www.musicminusone.com

Classic Arrangements
for Alto Saxophone

CONTENTS

ISBN 978-1-941566-91-6

MMO 12228

SOLO Eb ALTO SAXOPHONE

Teach Me Tonight

music by
Gene DePaul
lyrics by
Sammy Cahn

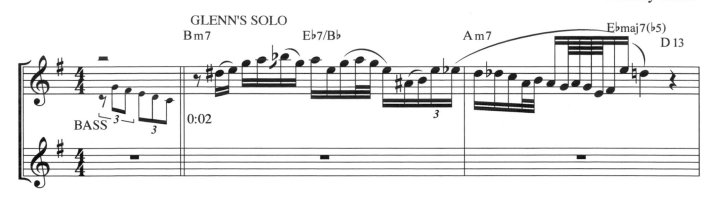

Did you say, I've got a lot to learn?

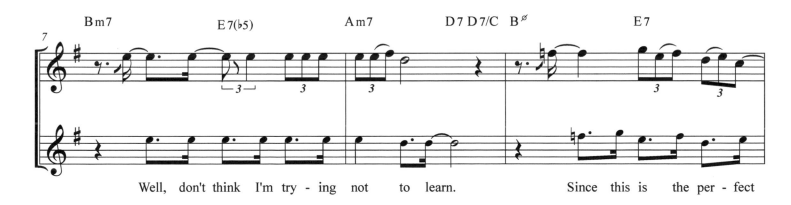

Well, don't think I'm try-ing not to learn. Since this is the per-fect

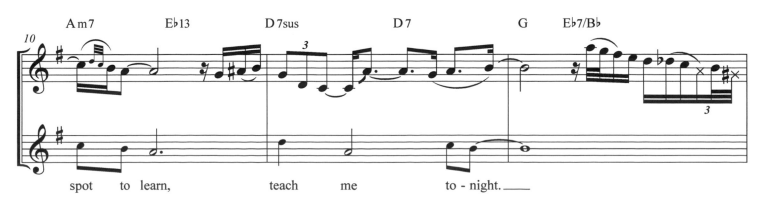

spot to learn, teach me to-night. ___

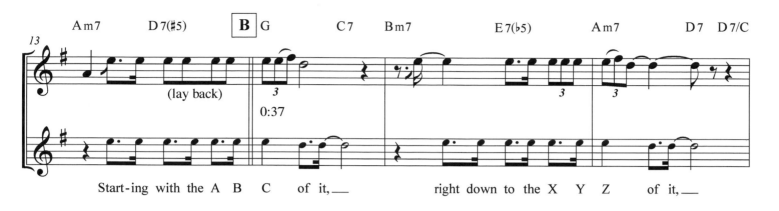

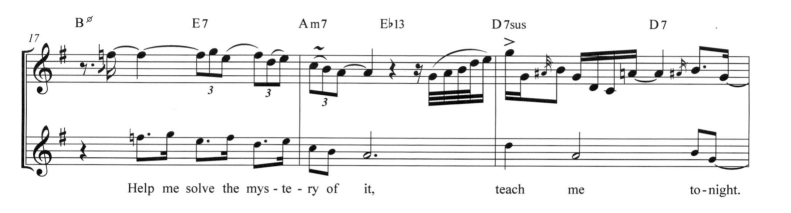

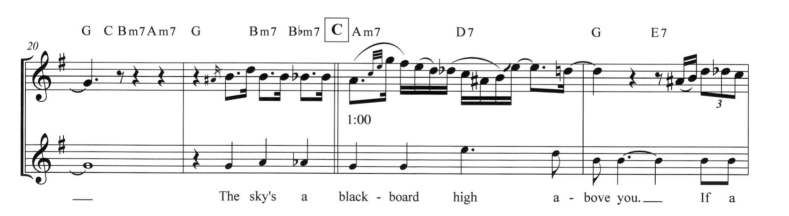

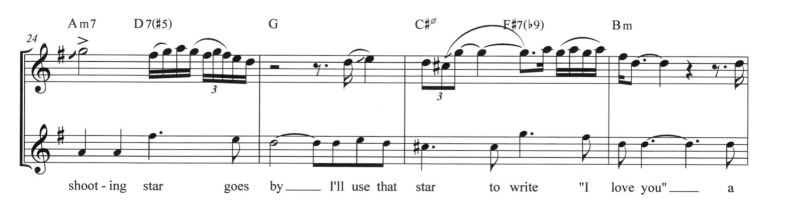

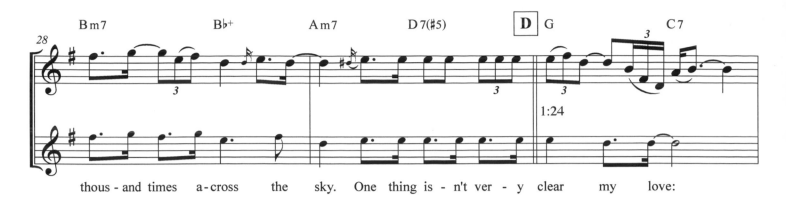

thous - and times a-cross the sky. One thing is-n't ver - y clear my love:

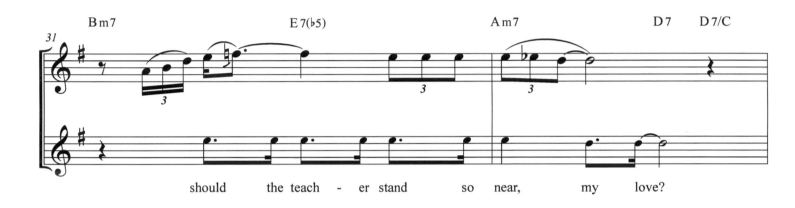

should the teach - er stand so near, my love?

Grad - u - a - tion's al - most here my love. Teach me to - night.

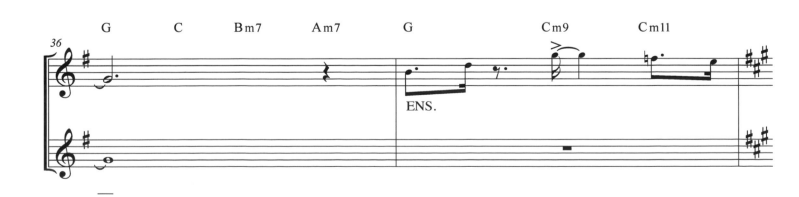

ENS.

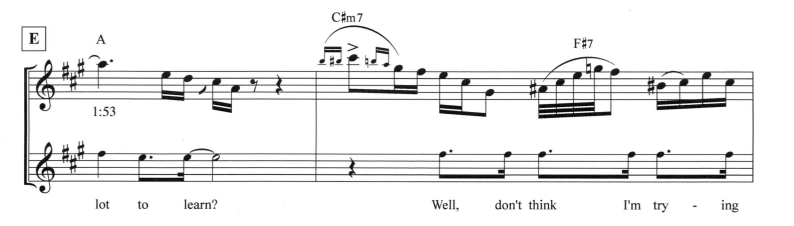

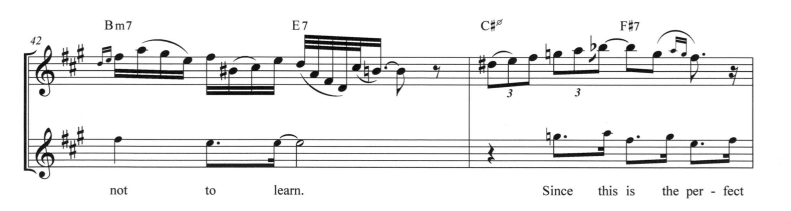

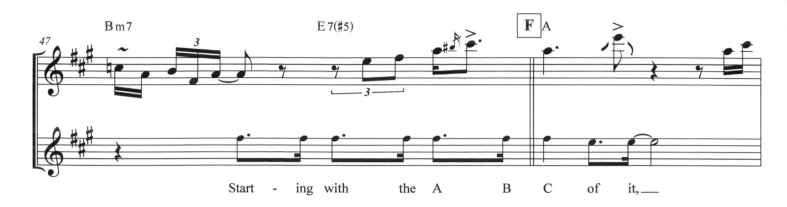

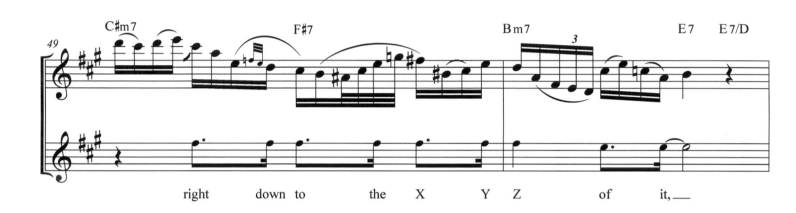

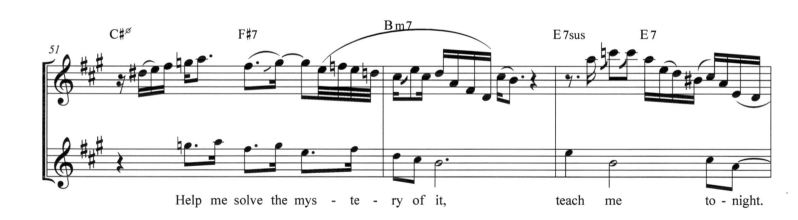

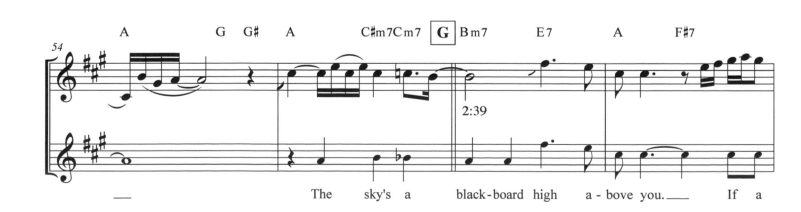

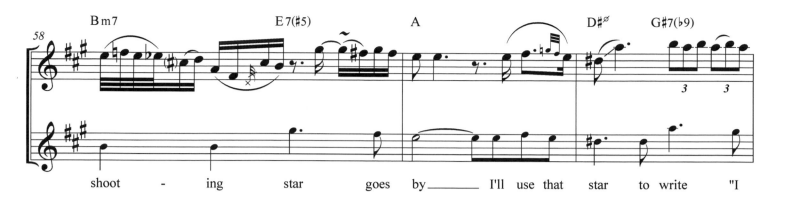

shoot - ing star goes by_____ I'll use that star to write "I

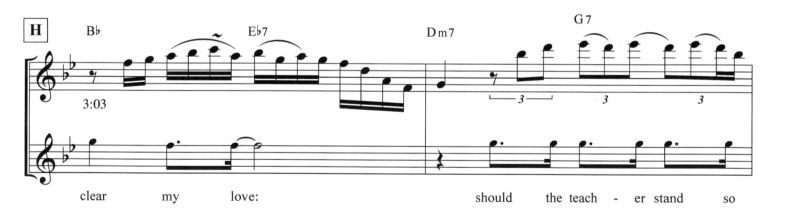

love you" _____ a thous - and times a-cross the sky. One thing is - n't ver - y

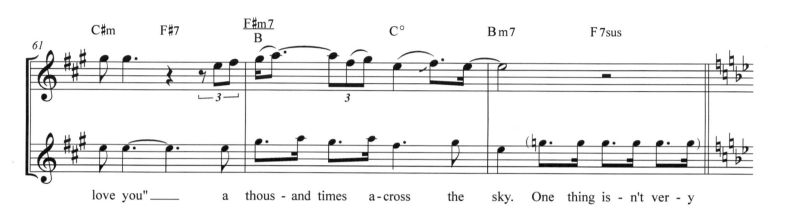

clear my love: should the teach - er stand so

near, my love? Grad - u - a - tion's al - most

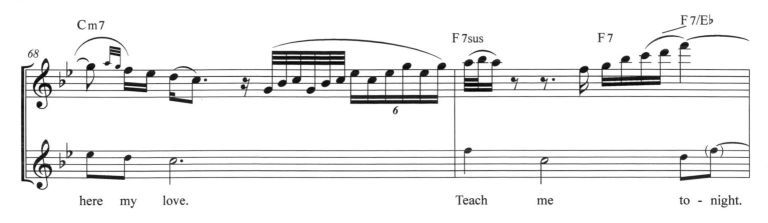

here my love.　　　　Teach　me　　　to - night.

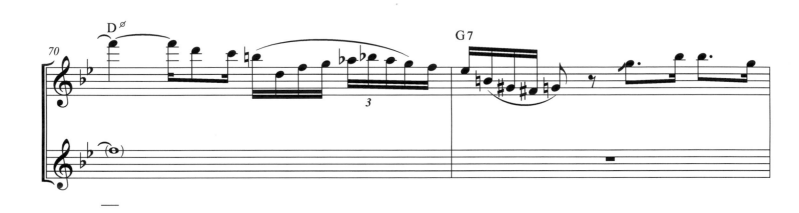

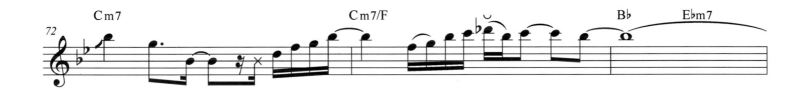

SOLO Eb ALTO SAXOPHONE

Angel Eyes

music by
Matt Dennis
lyrics by
Earl Brent

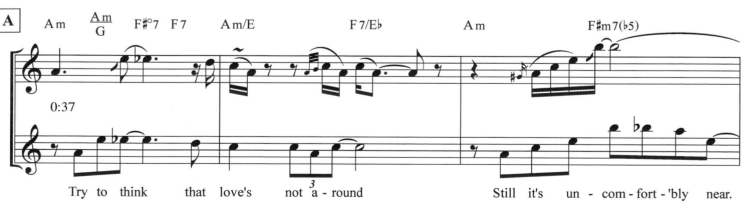

MMO 12228

My old heart__ ain't gain-in' no ground be-

cause my An-gel Eyes ain't here.__ An-gel Eyes__ that

old dev-il sent, they glow un-bear-a-bly bright.

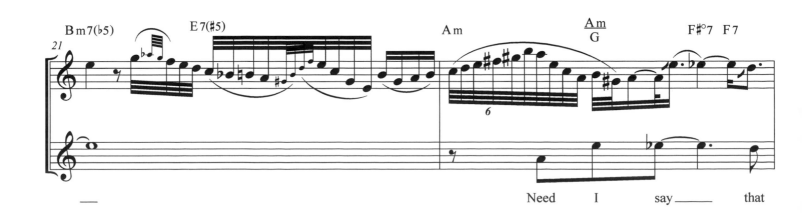

Need I say__ that

14

Par-don me____ but I got-ta run, the fact's un-com-mon-ly clear,

____ Got - ta find____ who's

now num-ber one____ and why my An - gel Eyes ain't here.____

MMO 12228

SOLO Eb ALTO SAXOPHONE

Come Rain Or Shine

music by
Harold Arlen
lyrics by
Johnny Mercer

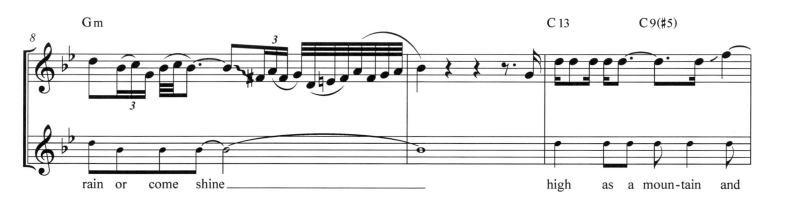

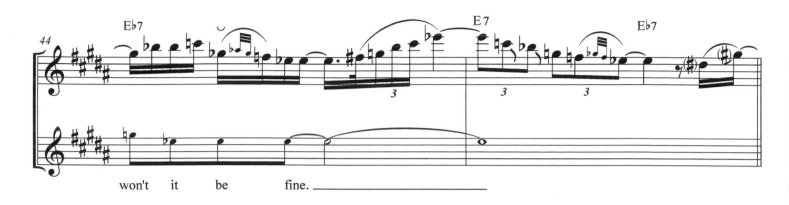

won't it be fine. _____

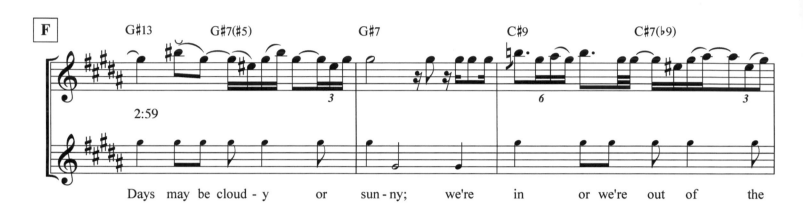

Days may be cloud-y or sun-ny; we're in or we're out of the

mon-ey. But I'm with you al-ways I'm with you rain or shine!

SOLO Eb ALTO SAXOPHONE

You Make Me Feel So Young

music by
Josef Myrow
lyrics by
Mack Gordon

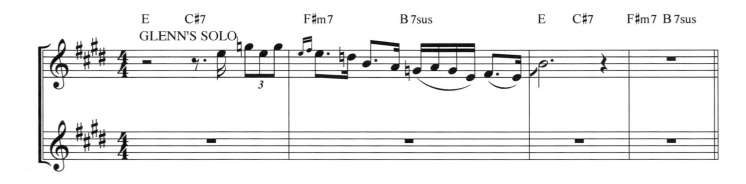

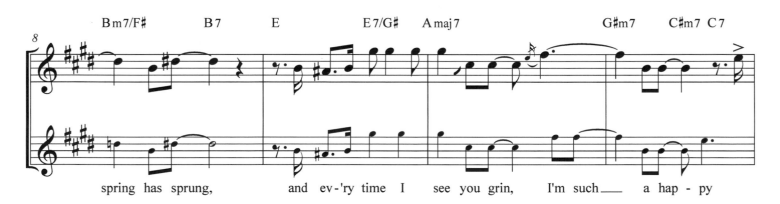

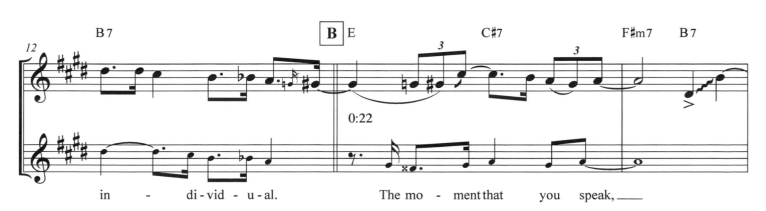

MMO 12228

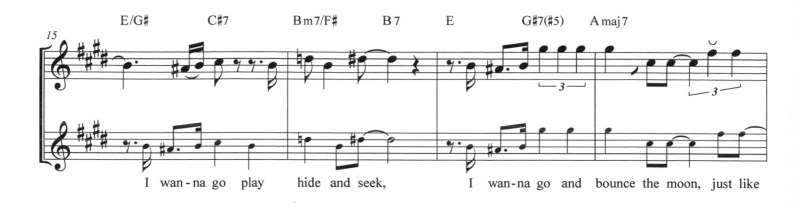

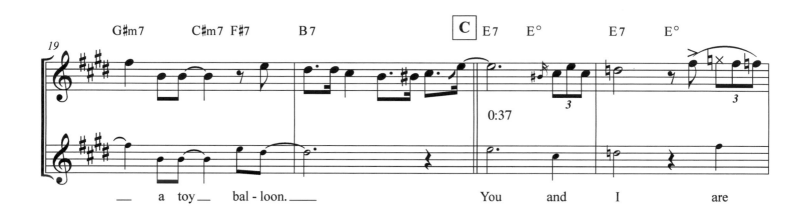

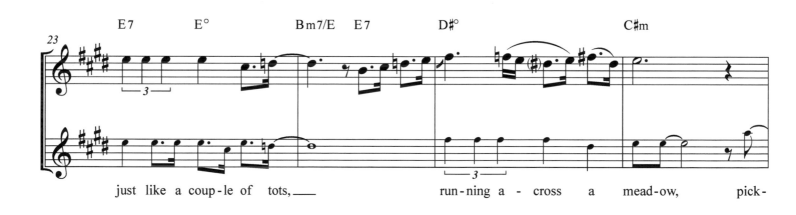

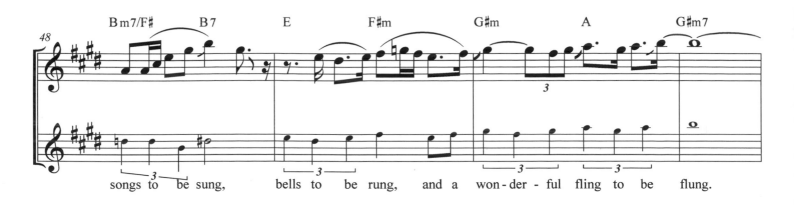

songs to be sung, bells to be rung, and a won-der-ful fling to be flung.

And e-ven when I'm old and gray, I'm gon-na feel the way I do to -

day, 'cause you make me feel so young.

1:47

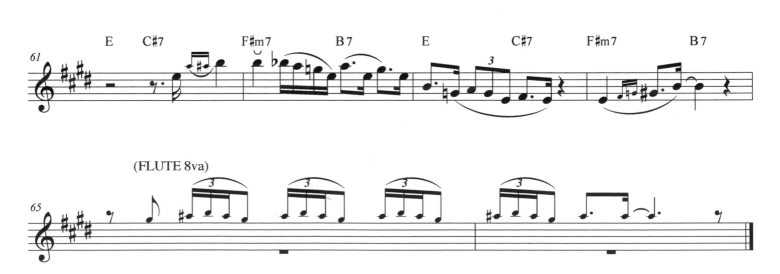

(FLUTE 8va)

SOLO Eb ALTO SAXOPHONE

Don't Worry 'Bout Me

music by
Rube Bloom
lyrics by
Ted Koehler

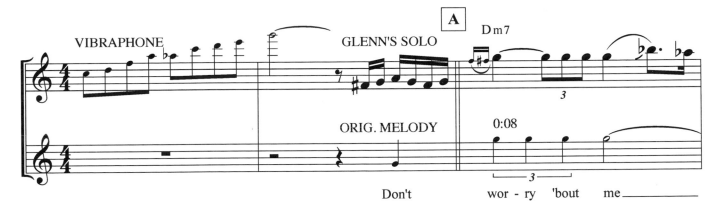

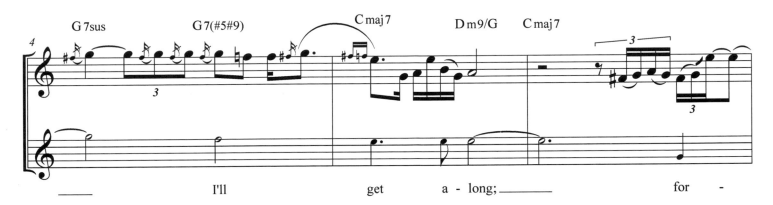

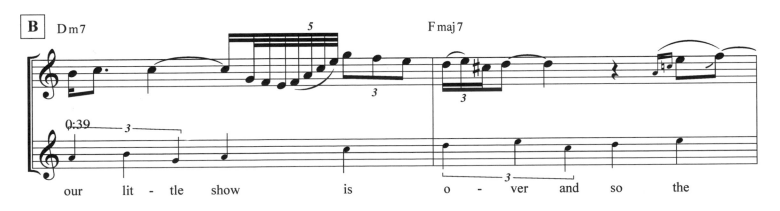

MMO 12228

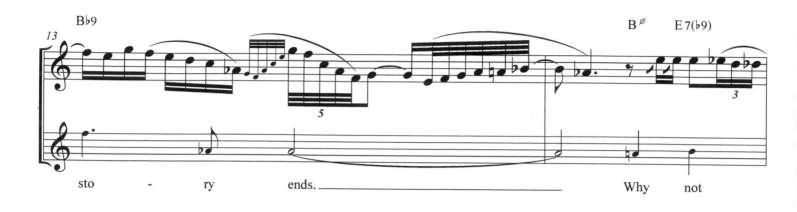

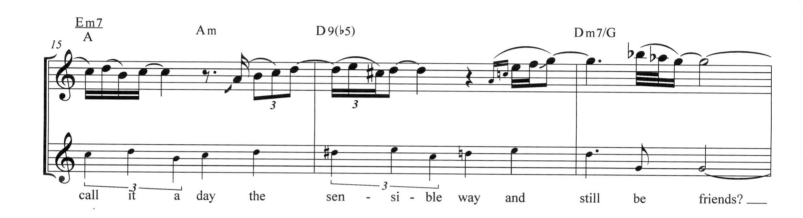

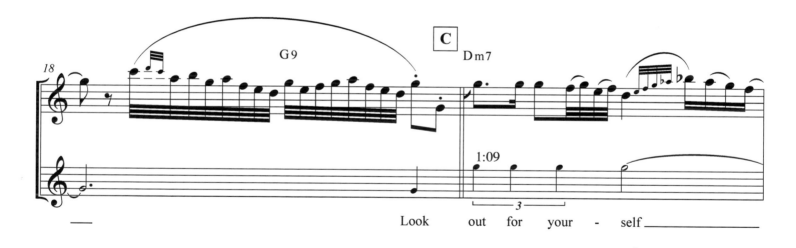

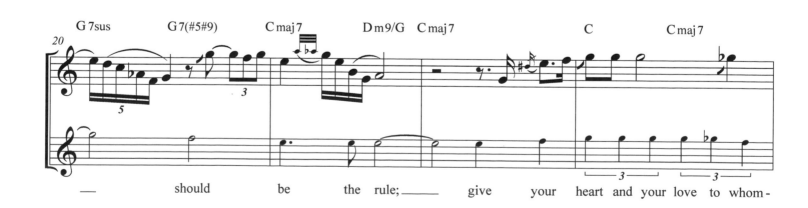

ev - er you love, don't be a fool. _____ Dar - ling,

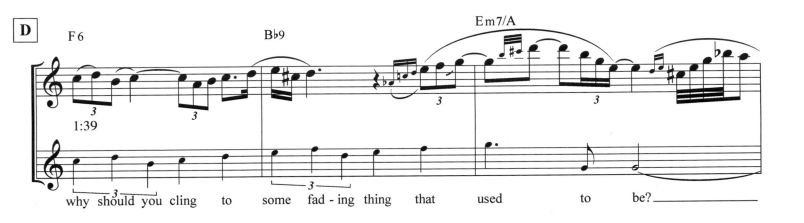

why should you cling to some fad - ing thing that used to be? _____

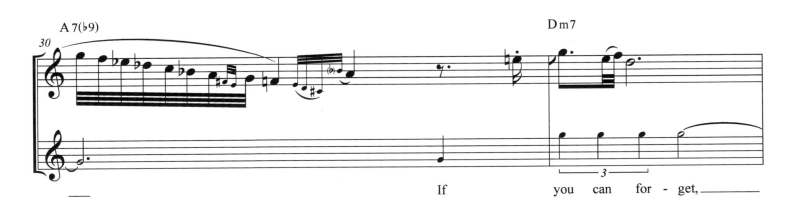

_____ If you can for - get, _____

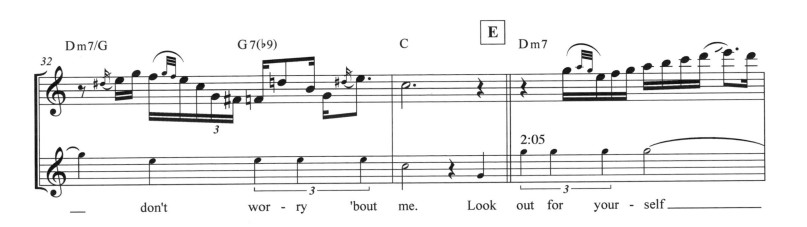

_____ don't wor - ry 'bout me. Look out for your - self _____

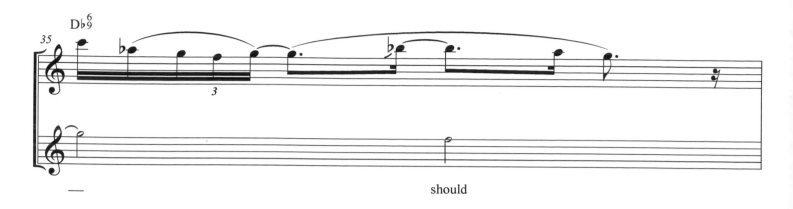

should

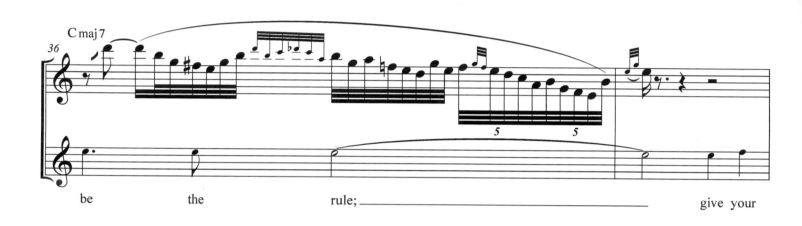

be   the   rule; _____ give your

heart   and   your love to whom - ev - er   you   love,   don't

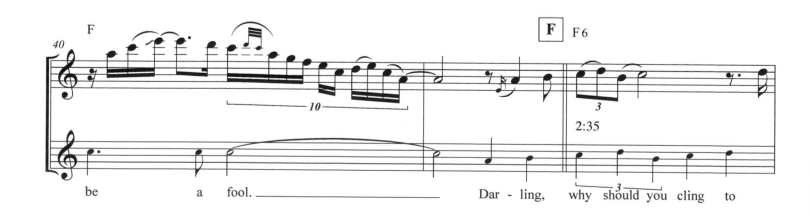

be   a   fool. _____ Dar - ling,   why should you cling   to

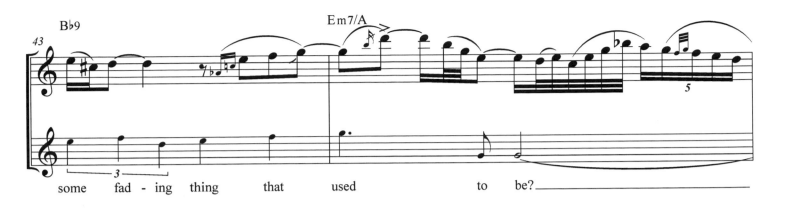

some fad - ing thing that used to be? _____

___ If you can for - get, ___ don't wor - ry 'bout

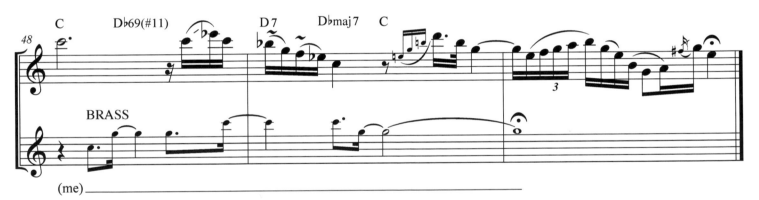

BRASS

(me) _____

SOLO Eb ALTO SAXOPHONE

Try A Little Tenderness

words and music by
Jimmy Campbell,
Reg Connelly and
Harry M. Woods

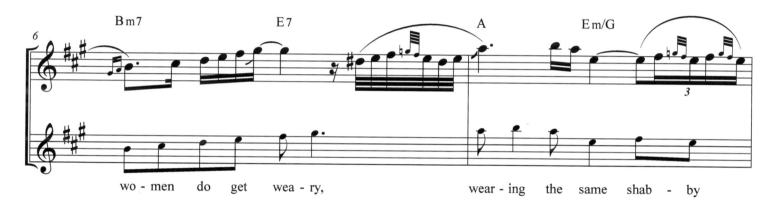

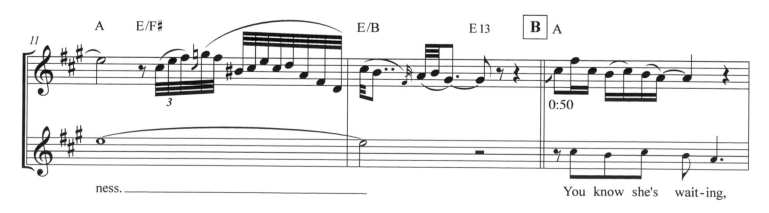

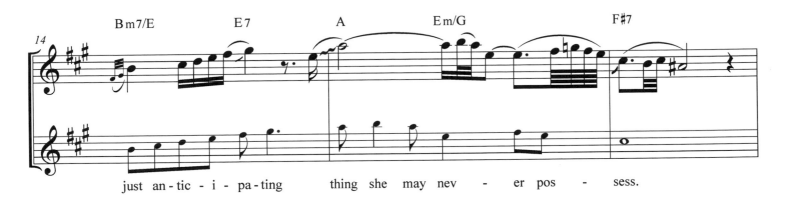

just an-tic-i-pa-ting   thing she may nev - er pos - sess.

While she's with-out them,   try a lit-tle ten - der - ness.

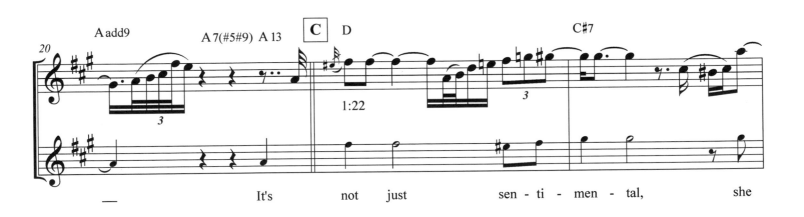

It's   not just   sen - ti - men - tal,   she

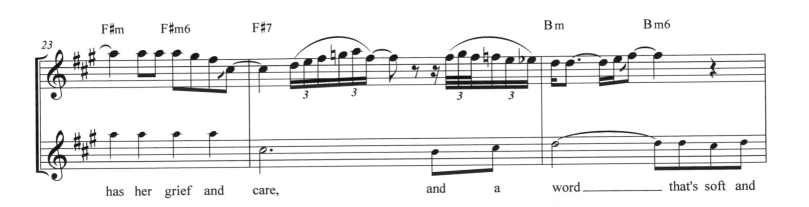

has her grief and care,   and a   word _____ that's soft and

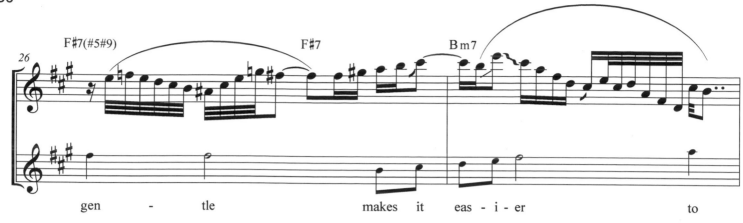

gen - tle   makes it eas - i - er   to

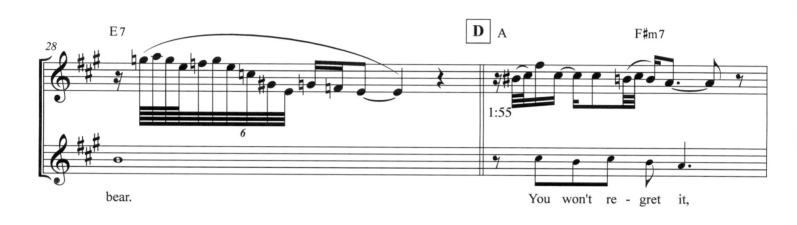

bear.   You won't re - gret it,

wo - men don't for - get it,   love is their whole hap - pi -

ness.   It's all so eas - y,   try a lit-tle ten - der -

ness.

SOLO Eb ALTO SAXOPHONE

If I Should Lose You

words and music by
Leo Robin and
Ralph Rainger

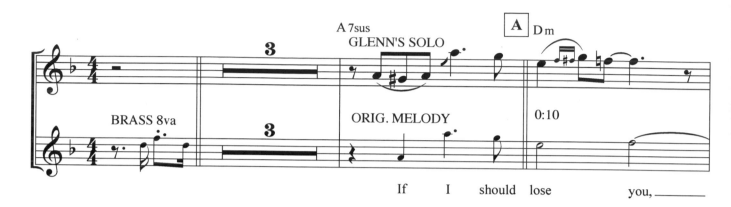

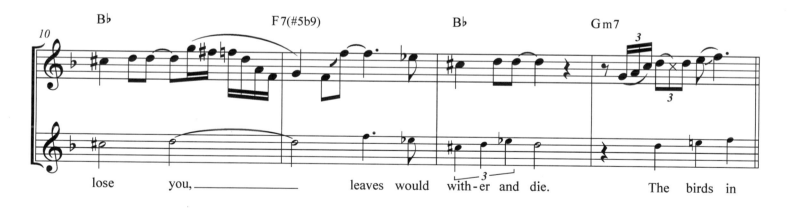

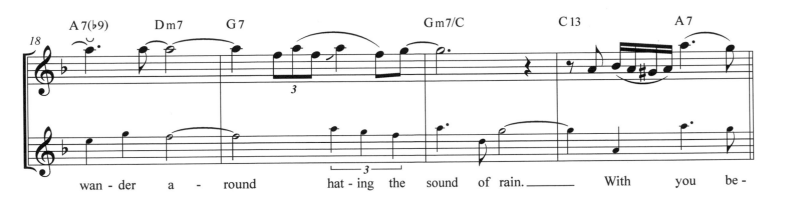

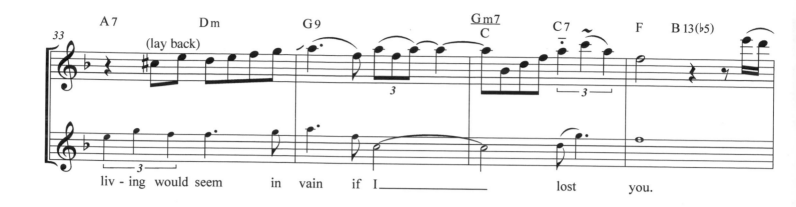

liv - ing would seem in vain if I _____ lost you.

If I should lose you, _____ the stars would

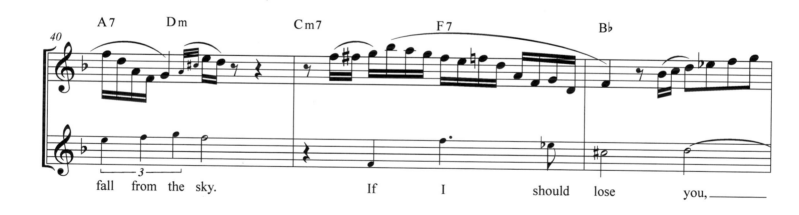

fall from the sky. If I should lose you, _____

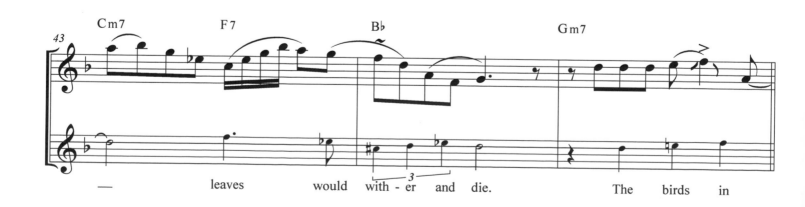

— leaves would with - er and die. The birds in

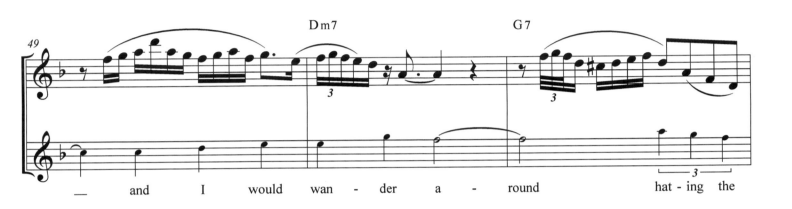

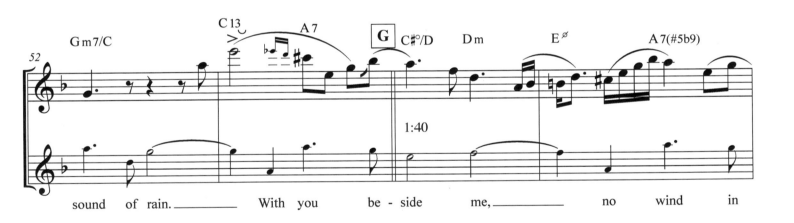

— a rose would bloom in the snow. I gave you

my love_____ and I was liv-ing a dream, but liv-ing would seem in vain if I

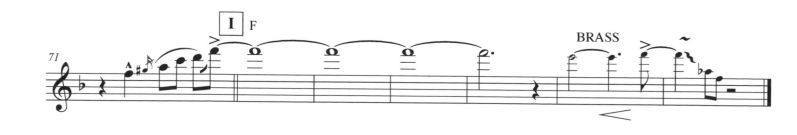

SOLO Eb ALTO SAXOPHONE

Autumn In New York

words and music by
Vernon Duke

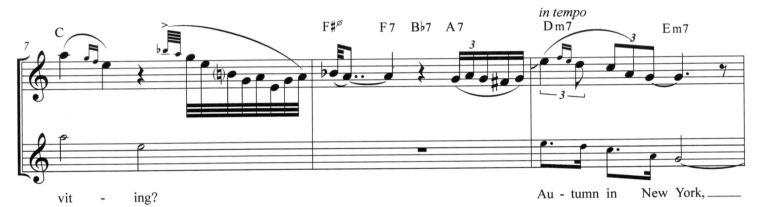

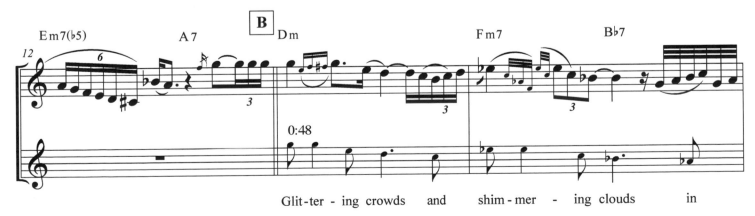

MMO 12228

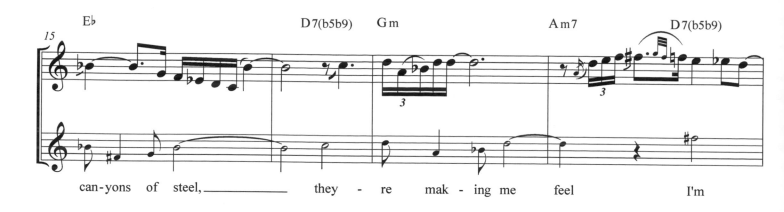

can-yons of steel,_____ they - re mak - ing me feel I'm

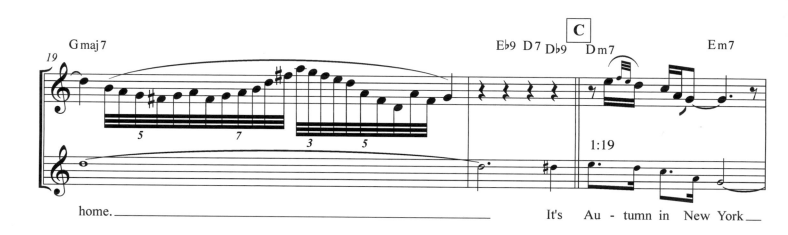

home._____ It's Au - tumn in New York __

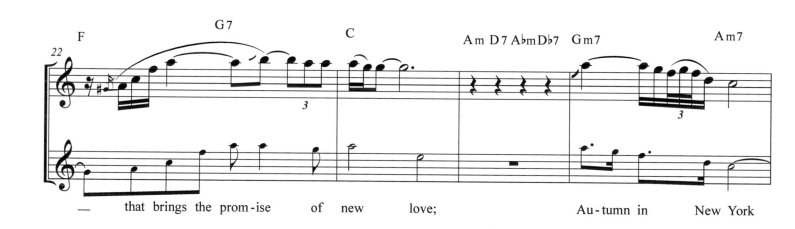

— that brings the prom-ise of new love; Au-tumn in New York

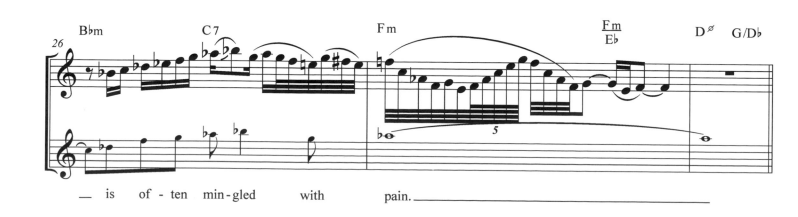

— is of - ten min-gled with pain.____

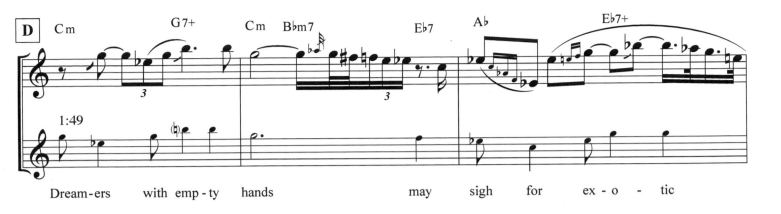

Dream-ers   with emp - ty   hands   may   sigh   for   ex - o - tic

lands;   it's   au - tumn in New York;____   it's   good to live it   a - gain.

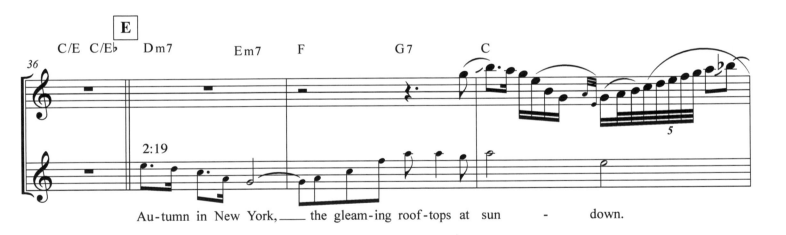

Au-tumn in New York,____ the gleam-ing roof-tops at sun - down.

Au-tumn in New York,____ it lifts you up when you're

40

run - down.   Jad - ed rou - es and

gay di - vor - cees who lunch at the Ritz_____ will

tell you that "it's____ di - vine!"_____

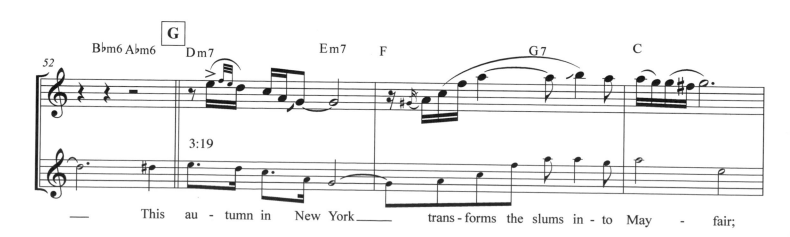

____ This au - tumn in New York____ trans - forms the slums in - to May - fair;

au - tumn in New York_____ you'll need no cas - tles in

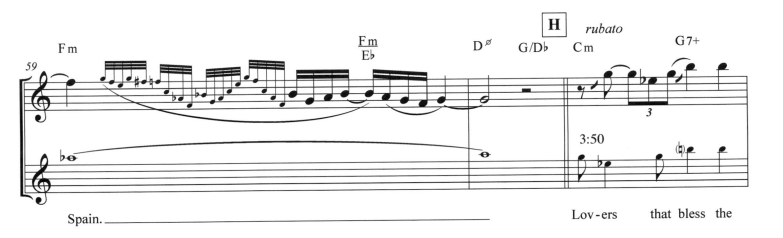

Spain._____ Lov - ers that bless the

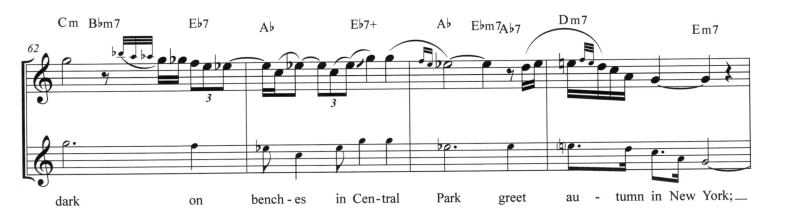

dark on bench - es in Cen - tral Park greet au - tumn in New York;__

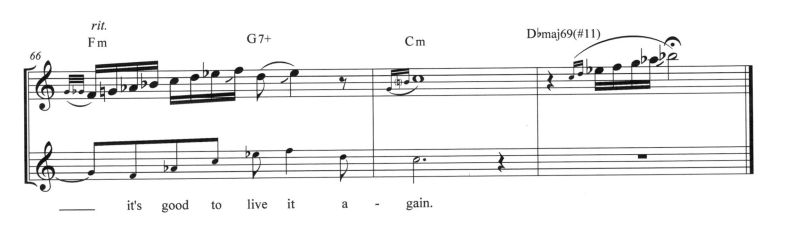

_____ it's good to live it a - gain.

SOLO Eb ALTO SAXOPHONE

Street Of Dreams

music by
Victor Young
lyrics by
Sam M. Lewis

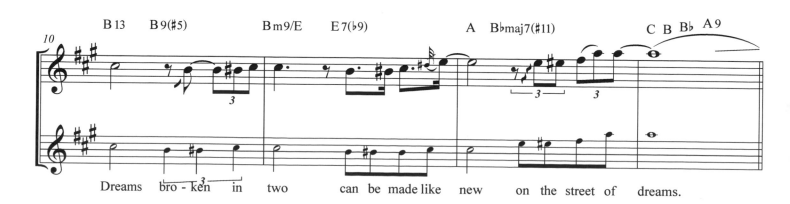

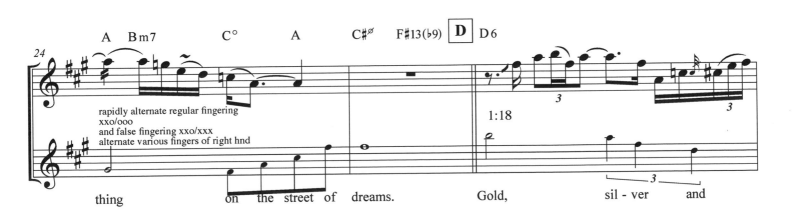

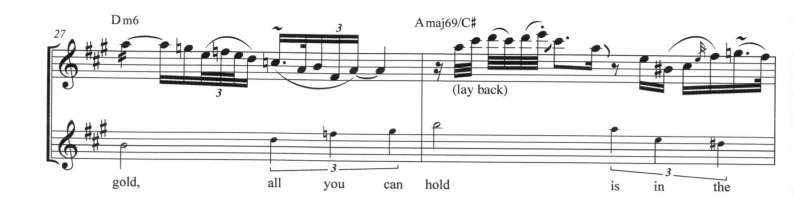

gold,   all   you   can   hold   is   in   the

moon -   beams.   Poor,   no - one   is   poor,   long as love is

sure   on   the   street   of   dreams.

Transcriptions by Mark Lopeman

Music Minus One 50 Executive Boulevard • Elmsford, New York 10523-1325
914-592-1188 • e-mail: info@musicminusone.com
www.musicminusone.com

MMO 12228

ISBN 978-1-941566-91-6